HOW TO MAKE MONEY FROM CRYPTOCURRENCY

Beginner's Guide To Cryptocurrency Investment

James Glean

TABLE OF CONTENT

CHAPTER ONE (1)

Introduction To Cryptocurrency

The world of finance is changing quickly, and cryptocurrency is a revolutionary force that is upending preconceived ideas about money and investing. The first and most well-known cryptocurrency, Bitcoin, sprang from the ashes of the 2008 financial crisis and helped create a whole new asset class. Thousands of digital currencies and blockchain initiatives are now part of the cryptocurrency industry, each with its own special attributes and profit-making possibilities. The appeal of cryptocurrencies is due to their novel technology as well as the possibility of large financial advantages. The public's fascination with tales of early Bitcoin adopters becoming millionaires almost overnight has fueled a gold rush mentality in the digital era. The road to bitcoin wealth is not easy to travel, though. The market is infamous for its extreme volatility, with prices that can jump or fall dramatically in a matter of hours.

The goal of this book is to demystify the cryptocurrency world and provide you the information and resources you need to successfully navigate this fascinating but challenging environment. Our aim is to provide you with techniques to possibly profit from this developing market while minimizing the inherent dangers, regardless of your level of familiarity with digital assets.

We'll look at a range of bitcoin income streams on these pages, from aggressive trading tactics to long-term investing plans. We'll examine the underlying technology of blockchain and clarify how various cryptocurrencies work. You'll discover how to utilize exchanges, set up safe wallets, and guard your digital assets against fraud and theft.

We'll also look at other ways to profit from the cryptocurrency ecosystem, like mining, staking, and taking part in decentralized finance (DeFi) systems. We'll also cover the important subject of taxes, assisting you in comprehending your responsibilities and figuring out how to maximize your returns while being compliant.

It's crucial to remember that there is a big chance of making money with cryptocurrencies, but there are also big hazards. This book will not hold back when addressing the difficulties and traps that await careless investors. We'll go over typical con games, how markets are manipulated, and how regulatory uncertainty may affect your investments.

You will have a thorough understanding of how to handle cryptocurrencies as a possible source of income by the time you finish reading this book. With this information at your disposal, you'll be more equipped to navigate the thrilling but sometimes stormy seas of the cryptocurrency world and make wise judgments. Never forget that in this quickly evolving world, education is your most valuable asset. Together, we can explore the possibilities of cryptocurrencies and learn how they could improve your financial situation in the future.

CHAPTER TWO (2)

What Is Cryptocurrency?

Cryptocurrency is defined as digital or virtual money that operates on a decentralised network called blockchain. Unlike fiat currencies, which are controlled and issued by central banks, cryptocurrency markets function independently of financial or governmental entities. An unidentified figure known only as Satoshi Nakamoto introduced Bitcoin, the first and most popular cryptocurrency, in 2009.

Numerous other cryptocurrencies with unique features and applications have been created since then.

The underlying technology of cryptocurrencies, cryptography regulates the creation of new units and secures transactions. This cryptography base makes transactions secure, unchangeable, and verifiable. As soon as a transaction occurs, it is broadcast to a network of computers known as nodes, and it is these nodes that verify and record the transaction on the blockchain, a public ledger. The distributed nature of cryptocurrency record-keeping makes it resistant to manipulation and fraud.

Blockchain technology is a novel concept in and of itself that underpins cryptocurrencies. It is essentially a sequence of blocks, each containing a list of transactions. Once a block is added to the chain, it cannot be deleted without affecting all subsequent blocks, requiring the consent of the majority of the network. As a result, logging transactions using blockchain technology is incredibly safe and transparent.

One of the main features of many cryptocurrencies is their limited supply. For example, the maximum quantity of Bitcoin is restricted to 21 million coins. The protocol is meant to produce scarcity, which is sometimes used as a metaphor for priceless metals like gold. There's a probability that the value will increase with time because to the limited supply and growing demand. However, this furthers the widely acknowledged volatility of bitcoin markets.

When contrasting traditional banking systems with cryptocurrency, several advantages may arise. Transactions can be conducted more rapidly and frequently for less money, especially for overseas transfers. Transactions provide some degree of pseudonymity because they are linked to cryptographic addresses rather than specific individuals. Additionally, cryptocurrencies have the potential to provide financial services to unbanked communities globally, as all that is needed to join is an internet connection and a digital wallet.

But cryptocurrencies also face significant challenges. The rapid fluctuations in their value make them risky investments. Due to the wide variances in national rules pertaining to cryptocurrencies, the market is unpredictable. Concerns have also been raised about the energy consumption of some cryptocurrency networks, particularly those like Bitcoin that use a Proof-of-Work consensus mechanism. Many people still think that cryptocurrencies will control the financial industry in the future, even in spite of these challenges. Within decentralised finance (DeFi) ecosystems, they can be utilised for anything from straightforward transactions to complex financial instruments.

CHAPTER THREE (3)

The Evolution Of Cryptocurrency

With the invention of Bitcoin in 2009 under the pseudonym Satoshi Nakamoto by an unidentified individual or group, cryptocurrency came into being. With the help of blockchain technology, Bitcoin created the first decentralised digital currency that runs on a peer-to-peer network and safely and openly records transactions. The goal of this invention was to develop a type of money that would let users to transfer funds directly to one another without the involvement of middlemen like banks or governments.

Developers started producing "altcoins," or alternative cryptocurrencies, as Bitcoin gained popularity. Litecoin and Namecoin are two notable instances of early prototypes that first surfaced in 2011. These alternative coins frequently aimed to enhance Bitcoin's interface or provide unique functionalities. With the introduction of smart contracts, which allowed for the development of decentralised apps (dApps) and opened the door to new use cases beyond straightforward currency transfer, Ethereum, which was introduced in 2015, saw a dramatic change.

With the advent of Initial Coin Offerings (ICOs) in 2017, the cryptocurrency ecosystem experienced fast expansion and a proliferation of new tokens and initiatives. Additionally, around this time there was a surge in speculative activity and public attention, which led to sharp price swings and regulatory scrutiny. Simultaneously, developments in technology tackled issues of scalability and energy efficiency. Examples of these include Ethereum's transition to a proof-of-stake consensus method and Bitcoin's Lightning Network.

Decentralised finance (DeFi), non-fungible tokens (NFTs), and central bank digital currencies (CBDCs) have all become more popular in recent years. While NFTs are used in digital art, gaming, and property rights, DeFi seeks to replicate traditional financial services in a decentralised fashion. A possible change in the global financial scene is being signalled by the fact that central banks and governments all over the world have started investigating or introducing their own digital currencies.

Key obstacles that still need to be overcome as cryptocurrencies develop are general acceptance, regulatory compliance, and environmental issues. Through technology advancements, self-regulation, and cooperation with governments and established financial institutions, the industry is attempting to address these problems. Future developments for cryptocurrencies could include more integration with current financial systems, creative uses of blockchain technology, and an ongoing reinterpretation of what value and money are in the digital era.

CHAPTER FOUR (4)

The Blockchain Technology Behind Cryptocurrency

The decentralised digital ledger known as blockchain technology, which powers cryptocurrencies, keeps track of transactions across a network of connected computers. Its structure, which consists of a series of blocks, each comprising a collection of transactions, is its primary innovation. A block's data becomes very difficult to change once it is added to the chain, offering a high level of security and transparency.

The consensus process used by the blockchain requires network users, or nodes, to confirm and agree upon the ledger's current state. For instance, the Proof-of-Work (PoW) consensus used by Bitcoin requires miners to compete by solving challenging mathematical puzzles in order to add new blocks. Alternative techniques for other cryptocurrencies could include Proof-of-Stake (PoS), which chooses validators according to the quantity of cryptocurrencies they own and are prepared to "stake" as collateral.

Blockchain's distributed nature is one of its key characteristics. The ledger is updated by a network of computers rather than a single entity. Due to the lack of a single point of failure, decentralisation improves security and fortifies the system against fraud and censorship. Additionally, it makes peer-to-peer transactions possible without the use of middlemen, which might save costs and boost productivity.

Blockchain technology has advanced to handle more complicated operations than just basic currency transfers. Smart contracts, which are self-executing contracts with stipulations encoded directly into code, have increased the potential of blockchain technology. Decentralised applications (dApps) have been developed as a result of this breakthrough, which was made possible by Ethereum and has created new opportunities in industries including finance, supply chain management, and digital identity verification.

As blockchain technology advances, it will encounter difficulties with energy consumption, scalability, and interoperability between various blockchain networks. Solutions including layer-2 scaling, more effective consensus techniques, and cross-chain communication protocols are being worked on by researchers and developers. By making blockchain technology more widely applicable, these developments hope to transform not only the financial industry but also a number of other areas of the global economy.

CHAPTER FIVE (5)

How To Get Started

Learn the fundamentals of cryptocurrencies before embarking on your trip. Learn about cryptocurrencies, blockchain technology, and the advantages and disadvantages that may arise. Learn about popular cryptocurrencies such as Ethereum and Bitcoin, and also become familiar with the idea of market volatility. Trustworthy books, websites, and learning environments can offer insightful content to expand your knowledge.

Next, select a trustworthy cryptocurrency exchange to trade, purchase, and sell digital assets. Kraken, Binance, and Coinbase are a few well-liked choices. Establish an account, carry out the required identity verification procedures, and make sure that robust security features like two-factor authentication are enabled. To gain a sense of comfort with the platform's functioning and interface, start with a little investment.

It's essential to store your cryptocurrency securely. Transferring greater holdings to a personal wallet is often safer, even though you can store smaller amounts on exchanges. Software wallets balance ease and security for frequent transactions, while hardware wallets give the highest level of protection for long-term storage. Look into several wallet possibilities and select one that fits your needs and level of technical comfort.

As your confidence grows, broaden your knowledge of other investment approaches. This could involve experimenting with more sophisticated choices like yield farming or staking, spreading your portfolio over several cryptocurrencies, or dollar-cost averaging (frequently investing tiny sums). But never forget that investing in cryptocurrencies carries a significant level of risk, so you should never take on more debt than you can afford to lose.

Lastly, keep yourself updated on the changing bitcoin scene. Join online forums, subscribe to reliable news sources, and stay up to date on legislative changes in your nation. Avoid con artists, pump-and-dump operations, and fictitious claims of rapid wealth. Success in the rapidly evolving realm of cryptocurrencies requires cautious engagement and continuous education as new opportunities and difficulties arise.

CHAPTER SIX (6)

Choosing A Cryptocurrency Exchange

For anyone wishing to venture into the realm of digital assets, choosing the appropriate cryptocurrency exchange is an essential first step. Start by assessing the security protocols and reputation of the exchange. Seek out exchanges with a solid security record, insurance against theft or hacking, and a track record of dependability. Industry rankings, security audit reports, and user reviews can offer important information about how reliable an exchange is.

Think about the variety of cryptocurrencies that are offered on the market. Popular coins like Bitcoin and Ethereum are usually available on large exchanges, but the one you choose may depend on your investing goals and level of interest in a particular altcoin. While some exchanges concentrate on a specific subset of cryptocurrencies, others cover a large range of them. Make sure the digital assets you want to trade are supported by the exchange. Take a close look at the exchange's fee schedule. Fees may include trading fees, deposit and withdrawal fees, and currency conversion costs. These can differ dramatically between platforms. Tiered charge structures based on trading volume or account balance are available on certain exchanges. Although cheaper prices are usually better, don't forgo features or security just to save money.

Evaluate the functionality and user interface of the exchange. Particularly for new users, a platform with easy-to-use navigation is crucial. Expert traders may provide preference to exchanges that provide complex instruments such as advanced order types, futures contracts, and margin trading. Think about whether the exchange offers customer service, market analysis, or educational materials to help you on your trading path.

Check to see if the exchange complies with any applicable laws in your area. Users are frequently better protected by regulated exchanges, which may also be compelled to follow stringent Know Your Customer (KYC) and Anti-Money Laundering (AML) protocols. These procedures help create a safer trading environment even if they can be time-consuming. Recognise any geographical limitations that can prevent you from accessing specific exchanges.

Finally, take into account the exchange's trading volume and liquidity.

It is usually easier to execute trades at specified price points when there is higher liquidity since tighter spreads and more stable prices follow. Examine the volume of daily trades in the cryptocurrencies that pique your interest on the exchange. Additionally, make sure the exchange accepts your preferred payment methods and has fair processing times by looking at the deposit and withdrawal choices.

CHAPTER SEVEN (7)

Setting Up A Digital Wallet

Transferring, receiving, and storing cryptocurrency all require a digital wallet. There are many different types of wallets, and each has a special convenience to security ratio. The two main kinds are cold wallets, which save data offline, and hot wallets, which store data online. Exchange wallets and software wallets are examples of hot wallets, whereas hardware wallets or paper wallets are considered cold wallets.

Setting up a software wallet starts with choosing a reliable wallet provider. Popular options include MetaMask for Ethereum and ERC-20 tokens, Exodus for numerous cryptocurrencies, and Electrum for Bitcoin. Download the wallet app from the official website or a reputable app store. Typically, the installation instructions ask you to create a new wallet or import a current one.

During the setup process, you will be provided with a recovery phrase, which is also referred to as a seed phrase. This phrase, which ranges from twelve to twenty-four words, is your wallet's backup. This phrase should never be saved digitally. Instead, write it down and store it someplace secure. Without this phrase, you won't be able to get your money back if you lose your wallet.

After configuring your wallet, ensure its security by selecting a strong password and activating any additional security features—like two-factor authentication—that are available. Certain wallets also allow you to link to hardware wallets or create multiple accounts, which further enhances security.

If you value the maximum level of protection, consider utilising a hardware wallet such as a Ledger or Trezor. Since your private keys are stored offline, it is incredibly difficult to hack these physical devices. You must connect the hardware wallet to your computer, install the necessary software, and adhere to the manufacturer's setup instructions in order to create or restore one.

Remember that regardless of the wallet type you select, the security of your bitcoin holdings ultimately depends on how well you protect your private keys and seed phrase. To guarantee you have the most recent security features, make sure your wallet software is up to date, never share it with anybody, and be cautious of phishing attempts.

CHAPTER EIGHT (8)

Understanding The Cryptocurrency Market

The cryptocurrency market is a complex, dynamic ecosystem that is impacted by numerous factors. Although supply and demand play a major role in how it operates, it differs from traditional financial markets in a few key ways. The global market is open 24/7 and is influenced by news regarding legislation, technological breakthroughs, and overall economic patterns.

Market capitalization is a crucial metric for understanding the current condition of cryptocurrencies. The answer is found by multiplying the total number of coins by the current price. The largest and most well-known cryptocurrency, Bitcoin, regularly dominates the market and has an impact on the whole sector. There are thousands of more cryptocurrencies on the market, frequently referred to as "altcoins," each with a different set of market dynamics and a business case.

Price volatility is one feature that distinguishes the bitcoin market. significant-scale, short-term price movements can be attributed to a number of factors, such as news stories, market sentiment, and significant trades. This volatility presents both possibilities and risks for investors. Having a firm grasp of concepts like trade volumes, market fluctuations, and support and resistance levels will help you navigate this turbulence more easily.

The cryptocurrency market is influenced by a wide range of players, including miners, developers, institutional investors, and individual investors. Changes in the market are significantly influenced by the interactions between these groups. Large institutional investments, for instance, may cause prices to rise, but large sell-offs or "dumps" may cause prices to fall precipitously.

When it comes to cryptocurrencies, market analysis usually combines technical and fundamental approaches. Fundamental analysis, which considers the project's technology, team, and real-world applications, looks at a cryptocurrency project's underlying value and potential. Technical analysis, on the other hand, employs price charts and statistical indicators to predict future price changes.

Lastly, it's imperative to understand how exchanges and market liquidity work. Arbitrage opportunities may arise from the same cryptocurrency being slightly more or less expensive on multiple exchanges. The degree of liquidity exhibited by various cryptocurrencies and exchanges might affect the ease of conducting transactions without causing a change in the market price.

CHAPTER NINE (9)

Major Cryptocurrencies And Their Features

The first and most well-known cryptocurrency is called Bitcoin (BTC). A proof-of-work consensus technology called Bitcoin was developed in 2009 and is sometimes referred to as "digital gold." Its primary characteristics are a 21 million currency maximum, pseudonymous transactions, and a decentralised network. Its main functions are that of a medium of exchange and a store of value.

Based on market capitalization, Ethereum (ETH) is the second-largest cryptocurrency. When smart contracts were introduced in 2015, Ethereum's architecture made it possible to create alternative cryptocurrencies and decentralised programmes (dApps). Ethereum is moving from proof-of-work to proof-of-stake consensus in an effort to save energy and increase scalability.

The native token of the Binance ecosystem, which is home to the biggest cryptocurrency exchange in the world, is called Binance token (BNB).

Token sales are made easier, trading expenses are reduced, and the Binance Smart Chain is powered by BNB. Using a proof-of-stake consensus mechanism, it periodically burns tokens to lower the total quantity accessible.

Cardano (ADA) is a proof-of-stake blockchain platform designed to rival Ethereum in the decentralised application hosting space. It places a strong emphasis on a development and sustainability strategy driven by research. Smart contracts are made feasible by the Cardano identity management and traceability framework.

The purpose of ripple (XRP) is to lower the cost and expedite international money transfers. Ripple is centralised and collaborates with reputable financial institutions, in contrast to a number of other cryptocurrencies. Rather than miners, a network of authorised validators validates XRP transactions.

Well-known for its speedy and affordable transactions is Solana (SOL), an innovative hybrid consensus mechanism that combines proof-of-stake and proof-of-history. Because of its scalability, it is utilised for NFT marketplaces and DeFi applications.

CHAPTER TEN (10)

Market Trends And Analysis

Market Cycles: Bull and bear markets are frequent occurrences in the bitcoin market. In contrast to bear markets, which are marked by falling prices and investor pessimism, bull markets are typified by rising prices and increased investor optimism. These cycles, which can extend for several months or years, are impacted by a number of variables, including modifications to laws and regulations, improvements in technology, and general economic conditions.

Volatility: Sharp swings are a well-known feature of cryptocurrency markets. Large-scale, transient price fluctuations are common and are typically triggered by noteworthy transactions, news stories, or shifts in market sentiment. Investors and traders face both opportunities and hazards as a result of this volatility.

Trends in Adoption: In the past few years, there has been a noticeable increase in the institutional acceptance of the bitcoin market. Major banks and organisations are starting to add Bitcoin and other cryptocurrencies to their treasury reserves as a means of guarding against inflation. This trend has contributed to the legitimacy and stability of the market.

Technological developments: New developments in technology have a big impact on the market. The price of individual cryptocurrencies as well as market trends may be significantly impacted by noteworthy breakthroughs in the fields of non-fungible tokens (NFTs), decentralised finance (DeFi), and layer-2 scaling approaches.

Regulatory Influence: The bitcoin market is still greatly impacted by developments pertaining to regulations. Important changes in the regulatory landscape of major economies or the introduction of new legislation could have a big impact on the markets. As the industry develops, more regulation is anticipated to become standard.

Techniques for Market Analysis: To comprehend and forecast changes in the market, analysts employ a variety of techniques. Technical analysis looks for patterns and trends in price charts and data indicators. A fundamental analysis evaluates a cryptocurrency project's intrinsic value by taking into account its team, technology, and practical applications. Blockchain data is subjected to on-chain analysis, which provides insights into investment behaviour and network activities.

CHAPTER ELEVEN (11)

Factors Influencing Cryptocurrency Prices

Supply and Demand: The basic elements influencing bitcoin values are supply and demand, just as in any other market. Price increases usually occur when there is a restricted supply (such as the 21 million coin restriction on Bitcoin) along with rising demand.

Conversely, lower costs may result from a decline in demand or an excess of supply.

Market Sentiment: Price fluctuations are significantly influenced by investor sentiment. Good news, technology developments, or increased use could increase demand and raise prices. Unfavourable incidents such as governmental actions, public protests, or security lapses may have the opposite impact.

Public Perception and Media Coverage: Both public perception and media coverage have a major impact on the price of bitcoin. Bad news might lead to sell-offs, while good news can also increase demand and draw in new investors. The opinions of influencers and social media debates also affect how the market responds to a product and how the general public perceives it.

Regulations: The values of cryptocurrencies are significantly influenced by laws and regulations imposed by the government. On the one hand, restrictive regulations or prohibitions may cause rapid price drops, while the adoption of supportive laws or institutional approval may result in price increases.

Macroeconomic Factors: The state of the world economy has an impact on cryptocurrency prices. Investors may turn to cryptocurrencies as a hedge due to concerns about inflation, falling currency values, and economic uncertainty, all of which could lead to price increases. On the other hand, strong traditional markets could discourage investors from making cryptocurrency investments.

Technological Advancements: New features or scaling solutions in blockchain technology could have a favourable effect on prices. Technical issues or security flaws, however, might result in lower expenses.

Market Manipulation: Due to its tiny size and lack of regulation, the bitcoin market is vulnerable to manipulation. Large purchasers or sellers (called "whales") have the ability to affect pricing. Artificial price movements can be produced by manipulative approaches such as pump and dump schemes.

Adoption and Integration: Prices may rise when more businesses, banks, or nations use the product. For instance, price increases typically occur when well-known businesses declare they will be investing in cryptocurrencies or taking bitcoin payments.

CHAPTER TWELVE (12)

Investment Strategies

HODLing, or Hold On for Dear Life: Purchasing cryptocurrency and holding it through market turbulence is the long-term approach. HODLers try to withstand short-term volatility because they think their investments have long-term potential.

Average Cost-Per-Item (DCA): DCA investors regularly purchase a certain amount of cryptocurrencies at any price. The long-term goal of this method is to reduce volatility and maybe the average cost per coin.

Increasing Portfolio Diversification: To reduce risk, this strategy distributes assets among a number of cryptocurrencies. Well-known coins like Ethereum and Bitcoin may be included in a diverse portfolio along with tokens and altcoins that have been carefully chosen from a range of companies.

Trade: Astute traders frequently buy and sell cryptocurrency in an effort to profit from brief price swings. This could involve trading in swings, days, or scalps. Compared to long-term investing, trading demands greater ability, patience, and risk tolerance.

Yield farming and staking: These tactics involve locking up cryptocurrency to generate passive income. offer farming can offer larger but more unpredictable returns in decentralised finance (DeFi) protocols, while staking often yields constant returns while maintaining proof-of-stake networks.

Investing through indices: The goal of this strategy is to place money into a collection of cryptocurrencies that, like traditional index funds, reflect the entire market or a particular sector. To complete the task, you have two options: employ bitcoin index funds or manually copy an index.

Remember that owing to market volatility, investing in cryptocurrencies carries a substantial risk. It's critical to finish your assignments, recognise your risk tolerance, and never invest more than you can afford to lose. Financial advisors should be consulted before making any significant investing decisions.

CHAPTER THIRTEEN (13)

Advanced Trading Techniques

Trading on margin entails borrowing money to expand the size of a trading position. It is capable of amplifying gains as well as losses. If the market goes against a trader's position, they need to be aware of the risk of liquidation.

Futures Trading: Traders who do not own the underlying asset can forecast future bitcoin prices. This allows for leverage as well as both long and short bets.

Trading Futures and Options: With options, traders have the

option—but not the responsibility—to purchase or sell an asset at a defined price. They can be applied to hedging or speculation.
In contrast to what was anticipated

This entails taking advantage of variations in currency prices. Traders win when they buy on one exchange and sell on another. It requires quick execution and perhaps complex software.
Trading grids: a method that regularly executes several buy and sell orders above and below the current price. It seeks to make money when prices move inside a range.
Cut Down

This is a significant amount of trading to take advantage of minor price changes. Accurate performance and prompt decision-making are required.
Using computer software to carry out trades automatically in accordance with preset criteria is known as algorithmic trading. Strategies for high-frequency trading may be part of this.
Sentiment analysis is the process of examining news, social media, and market data to forecast price changes and assess sentiment in the market.
Analysis at the Chain Level: looking through blockchain data to learn more about whale movements, network activity, and other factors that can affect prices.
Dealing in Pairs: To profit from a shift in the price relationship between two linked cryptocurrencies, one must take opposite positions in each.

These methods typically carry a larger risk and need specialised equipment, technological expertise, and in-depth knowledge of the sector. They might not be appropriate for novice traders and are usually utilised by seasoned traders. Before putting a strategy into practice, make sure you fully understand it and take your risk tolerance into account.

CHAPTER FOURTEEN (14)

Technical Analysis For Cryptocurrency

In order to forecast future market moves, technical analysis in cryptocurrency trading examines past price data and volume. Among its core beliefs are the notions that prior price patterns frequently recur and that market psychology affects trading decisions.
The following are some essential elements of technical analysis:

Chart Patterns: Traders can recognise patterns like as triangles, flags, head and shoulders, and double tops and bottoms. These tendencies might indicate the start or continuance of a trend.
Trend lines: To show the general direction of the price, these are made by joining a sequence of highs or lows. Trend lines are used by traders to determine levels of support and resistance.
Moving averages: They smooth out price data and draw attention to trends over predetermined time periods. The Simple Moving

Average (SMA) and the Exponential Moving Average (EMA) are two often utilised types. Trend shifts can be indicated by crossovers between various moving averages.

Oscillators: These indicators aid in determining whether the market is overbought or oversold. The relative strength index (RSI) and the stochastic oscillator are two common oscillators.
Volume: Trends can be confirmed or possible reversals can be detected by comparing trading volume to price changes.

Fibonacci Retracements: These levels are utilised to determine probable levels of support and resistance because they are based on the Fibonacci sequence.
Candlestick Patterns: Traders can create patterns that indicate sudden changes in price by mixing individual and group candlesticks.
The Bollinger Band is a useful tool for measuring volatility and spotting possible breakouts. They are made up of a moving average with upper and lower bands based on standard deviation.
The Moving Average Convergence Divergence, or MACD, indicator can be used to spot shifts in momentum by displaying the connection between two moving averages.

Traders will occasionally combine various indicators and tools to get a complete view of the state of the market. It's critical to remember that technical analysis is a useful but not perfect method. News events, market emotion, and other external variables can overpower technical indicators.

CHAPTER FIFTEEN (15)

Volatility And Market Manipulation

Unpredictable actions: The volatility of cryptocurrency markets is well recognised. Significant price movements often happen faster and more violently than in traditional financial markets.

Market Size: Because the cryptocurrency market is smaller than traditional markets, it is more susceptible to large price swings.
Liquidity: Cryptocurrencies with limited liquidity are more likely to see significant price fluctuations during major transactions.
Speculation: A large portion of trade is speculative, which can lead to sudden mood swings.
News Sensitivity: The value of cryptocurrencies usually fluctuates significantly in reaction to breaking news, governmental decrees, or technological advancements.
Trading Around the Clock: Because cryptocurrency exchanges are available around-the-clock, unlike traditional markets, price volatility is always conceivable.

Trickery of the Market: Because of its decentralised nature and relative absence of regulation, the bitcoin market is open to a range of manipulation techniques.

Pump and dump schemes are organised attempts to inflate the price of a cryptocurrency before dumping it for a profit (pump).
Whale Manipulation: Big holdings, or "whales," have the power to significantly influence prices by executing enormous purchase or sell

orders.

Wash Trading: An artificial trading volume is produced when two individuals purchase and sell the identical asset at the same time.

The act of making large orders with no intention of fulfilling them in order to manipulate supply and demand perceptions is known as spoofing.

FOMO: The dissemination of misleading information or exaggerated claims intended to engender FOMO (fear of missing out) or FUD (fear, uncertainty, and doubt).

Front-running is the practice of executing transactions using insider information before significant orders or announcements.

Market making: This tactic is sometimes used by large dealers or exchanges to influence prices.

The decentralised structure of bitcoin exchanges and their global reach make enforcement difficult, but regulators throughout the world are becoming more aware of these strategies. Investors should conduct in-depth research and be aware of these risks prior to making an investment.

CHAPTER SIXTEEN (16)

Earning Passive Income With Cryptocurrency

The ability of cryptocurrencies to yield passive income has simplified the process of growing digital assets without the need for constant active trading. One of the most common strategies is staking, or locking up your money to guarantee the safety and smooth operation of a blockchain network. In return, you receive rewards in the form of additional funds. For proof-of-stake cryptocurrencies like Ethereum 2.0, Polkadot, and Cardano, this tactic is highly well-liked. Because staking can sometimes be done directly through cryptocurrency wallets or exchanges, even beginners can participate in it.

Another well-known strategy in the decentralised finance (DeFi) ecosystem is yield farming. This means providing liquidity to decentralised lending exchanges or protocols. By putting your cryptocurrency assets in liquidity pools, you can earn extra reward tokens and a share of the platform's transaction fees. Even because give farming may yield better returns than staking, there is a greater chance of loss due to the potential for smart contract errors and temporary loss.

Lending platforms present a different approach to making passive income. Using regulated markets like BlockFi and decentralised networks like Aave, you can lend your bitcoin holdings to borrowers in return for interest payments. Stablecoins can produce more consistent returns even though their value may be lower. Interest rates are subject to significant fluctuations based on the cryptocurrency and market conditions.

Those who can afford them can find that a masternode is a very valuable passive income stream. Certain nodes, also known as masternodes or complete nodes, perform specialised functions in some bitcoin networks, such as expediting transactions or voting on submitted proposals for governance. Even though starting a masternode frequently requires a substantial initial expenditure and a high level of technical competence, it is possible for it to eventually produce continuous income.

Lastly, certain tokens and cryptocurrencies offer their holders advantages that are similar to dividends. These might be profit-sharing tokens, which split a percentage of platform earnings, or governance tokens, which encourage holders to engage in the ecosystem. This approach can be profitable, but it requires a great deal of investigation to identify trustworthy businesses that employ eco-friendly distribution methods.

Conclusion: The Future Of Cryptocurrency

It seems probable that bitcoin will see increased usage and integration into the global financial system in the future. We may see a greater acceptance of cryptocurrencies for everyday transactions, money transfers, and value storage as institutional investors and the general public become more knowledgeable about digital assets. User interface improvements could accelerate its adoption by simplifying cryptography for non-technical users.
The degree of regulatory certainty is expected to have a significant influence on the growth of the bitcoin market. Governments and financial organisations may be able to achieve a compromise between innovation and consumer protection while more comprehensive legislation for digital assets are implemented. This could lead to a rise in institutional participation and the development of more sophisticated financial products like derivatives and exchange-traded funds (ETFs) for cryptocurrencies.

Continued technological advancements will be the driving force behind the rise of cryptocurrencies. Blockchain technology needs to be enhanced in terms of scalability, energy efficiency, and multi-network interoperability in order to address current problems. The landscape of bitcoin may be significantly impacted by the creation of layer-2 solutions and the anticipated broad adoption of central bank digital currencies (CBDCs).

It is anticipated that cryptocurrencies will be significantly impacted by future advancements in decentralised finance, or DeFi. As these protocols advance and become more broadly accessible, they have the potential to completely transform the lending, insurance, and banking industries. Additionally, they could offer moderately priced substitutes for well-known financial services. Combining real-world assets with DeFi systems may be one strategy to bridge the divide between traditional banks and the cryptocurrency industry.

Environmental and sustainable concerns will probably have an impact on the development of cryptocurrencies in the future. Less energy-intensive consensus techniques could become commonplace, with proof-of-stake potentially acting as the benchmark. In addition to tackling global concerns like supply chain openness, digital identity management, and enabling more effective governance systems, blockchain technology and cryptocurrencies may be very beneficial.